I0108139

SHAKESPEARE
THY NAME IS
MARLOWE

Other books by David Rhys Williams:

FAITH BEYOND HUMANISM

WORLD RELIGIONS AND THE HOPE FOR PEACE

A reproduction of the portrait, recently discovered at Corpus Christi College, Cambridge, England, which many believe to be an authentic portrait of Christopher Marlowe at the age of 21. Used by permission of the Master and Fellows of Corpus Christi College.

Shakespeare Thy Name Is Marlowe

By David Rhys Williams

Philosophical Library　　　　　*New York*

Copyright, 1966, by Philosophical Library, Inc.
15 East 40 Street, New York 16, N. Y.

Library of Congress Catalog Card Number: 66-16173

All rights reserved

ISBN 978-0-8065-3015-4

Printed in the United States of America

A new scientific truth does not triumph by convincing its opponents and enabling them to see the light, but rather because its opponents eventually die and a new generation grows up that is familiar with it.

—MAX PLANCK[1]

FOREWORD

A special interest in Christopher Marlowe, the brilliant dramatist of the Elizabethan era, began for me in high school with a teacher of English who stressed the importance of Marlowe's poetic and pioneering genius. She lamented his early death at the age of 29 and stimulated in at least one of her pupils an enduring curiosity concerning the mysterious circumstances surrounding it.

This curiosity was further stimulated by a lecture given in Cleveland, Ohio, in the spring of 1923 by a distinguished American scientist who offered some evidence that Marlowe must have lived beyond the date of his alleged murder, and that either he was Shakespeare or closely cooperated with him.

Then, several years later, there were published two books, one in 1955 and the other in 1956, which greatly quickened my interest in the controversial issue; for both made plausible claims for Marlowe's authorship, not only of the works commonly attributed to him, but also of the plays and sonnets included in the First Folio of Shakespeare.

In the spring of 1959, my wife and I took a trip to England primarily to get in touch with members of the Marlowe Society, whose London Chapter I was invited to address soon after our arrival, at the gracious suggestion of Calvin Hoffman, the American poet and playwright.

Later we visited many of the shrines sacred to the

memory of Marlowe, such as the Cathedral School in Canterbury, where he came to the notice of the Archbishop; Corpus Christi College in Cambridge, where he received his Bachelor's and Master's degrees; Scadbury, the large estate in Chislehurst, where he lived for sometime as the protege of Thomas Walsingham; the Anchor in Bankside, London, which replaced the original tavern where Marlowe and his fellow dramatists were accustomed to gather; and the church in Deptford which has preserved a record of his death and burial. Of course, we also visited the shrines at Stratford-on-Avon.

When we were in Canterbury, Dr. William Urry, archivist for both the Cathedral and the City, showed us a carton containing (we understood him to say) over 500 newly discovered documents concerning Marlowe, either directly or indirectly, many of which identified him as Shakespeare. I have been eagerly looking forward to the publication of a comprehensive report on these documents as Dr. Urry then planned, but we have learned since that illness has delayed the project.

Now I do not claim to be either a Marlovian or a Shakespearean expert. An expert knows his subject from "A to Z." My knowledge of my subject is primarily from "M to S," from Marlowe to Shakespeare, and it goes without saying that there are large gaps even in this knowledge. It would therefore be more accurate to claim merely a sustained interest in the mystery involved and a mounting faith that in searching for the solution, the search itself is at long last on the right scent.

DAVID RHYS WILLIAMS

Rochester, New York

8

CONTENTS

Chapter I

WHO WAS SHAKESPEARE?

The 400th anniversary of the birth of the William Shakespeare, who is buried in Stratford-on-Avon, was widely celebrated throughout the world even though his authorship of the literary works commonly attributed to him has not been established beyond a reasonable doubt. In fact, his authorship is more cogently disputed today than at any time since it was first alleged.

While it is true that the great majority of the professors and teachers of English literature still accept the man from Stratford as the authentic author, with or without reservations, it is the creative literary artists, knowing what is involved in producing literature of high quality, who seriously question the claim made in his behalf.

Henry James has said, "I am sort of haunted by the conviction that the divine William was the biggest and most successful fraud ever practiced on a patient world."[2]

The distinguished editor and scholar, Henry Watterson, has said, "The man who can believe that William Shakespeare of Stratford-on-Avon wrote the dramas that stand in his name could believe that Benedict Arnold wrote the Declaration of Independence and Herbert Spencer the novels of Dickens."[3]

Mark Twain wrote in reference to Shakespeare: "About him you can find nothing. We can go to the records and find out the life history of every renowned horse of modern times, but not Shakespeare. There are many reasons for this, but there is one worth all the rest put together—he hadn't any history to tell." Of course, Mark Twain must have meant that "he hadn't any *literary* history to tell," for there are records of his baptism, marriage, law suits, real estate transactions, children, last Will and Testament, and death and burial, but no records of his ever having written any of the dramas which bear the name of Shakespeare.

Nathaniel Hawthorne, Ralph Waldo Emerson, Walt Whitman, Oliver Wendell Holmes, John Greenleaf Whittier, Sigmund Freud, Lord Palmerston, Prince Bismarck —all of these took the position that there was something incredible and absurd about the Shakespeare authorship.[3] They have agreed on only one point—not who the author was but who he could not have been.

The genius who wrote those magnificent plays and sonnets was not only a brilliant mind but a highly educated person—either college-educated or self-educated. Also, he must have moved freely in the highest court circles at one time or another, travelled on the continent of Europe, and at least visited Italy.

But there is no documentary evidence to show that the Shakespeare of Stratford possessed a common school education or even owned a book or could have had a

12

fighting chance to educate himself outside of a college, because there were no public libraries in his day, no published grammars, no dictionaries as in the days of Abraham Lincoln (who had been able to educate himself by such means).

Almost all the books which the author of those plays would have had to read to be self-educated were at Oxford and Cambridge Universities, where they were fastened down by chains to reading desks from which the general public was rigorously excluded—such books in those days were as precious as jewels. They were open only to formally registered students. There is no documentary record of the Shakespeare from Stratford as having been among those so registered. What about access to the private libraries of the rich and the influential? There is likewise no documentary evidence that he ever had any such access. All the biographies which credit him with an education are based on speculation.[4]

In five of the six authentic signatures we have of this man, his name is spelt Shakper, in one Shakspe. There are authentic references to him in which his name is variously spelt Shaxper, Shagsper, and Shacksper, but none of the signatures or references has the same spelling as the name printed in the First Folio.

In the *Cambridge History of English Literature,* issued in 1910 from the very heart of conservative England, we have the following statement regarding the Shakespeare of Stratford:

> We do not know the identity of Shakespeare's father; we are by no means certain of the identity of his wife. . . . We do not know whether he ever went to

13

school. No biography of Shakespeare, therefore, which deserves any confidence has ever been constructed without a large infusion of the tell-tale words "apparently," "probably," "there can be little doubt," and no small infusion of the still more tell-tale "perhaps," "it would be natural," "according to what was usual at the time," etc. etc.[5]

In 1620 Ben Jonson made a list of the distinguished persons he had known. It contained no mention of anyone by the name of Shaksper or Shakespeare. Then, within three years, the First Folio was published containing his enthusiastic and lyrical praise of the "Soul of the Age," "Star of Poets," "Sweet Swan of Avon." (See Appendix VI).

In a description of Stratford, published in 1645, there is included the following:

> Stratford owes all its glory to two of its sons—John, Archbishop of Canterbury, who built a church there; and Hugh Clopton who built at his own cost a bridge of fourteen arches across the Avon.

In commenting on this paragraph, Dr. Thomas C. Mendenhall, at one time Professor in Ohio State University, writes, "The church referred to is that containing Shakespeare's tomb and also those of the Clopton family. The citation is evidence that 29 years after his death, and 22 years after the publication of the complete First Folio edition of his works, Shakespeare was not considered an asset in the town in which he was born and which today . . . lives and feeds upon his memory. Evidently the myth had not yet started on its triumphant way."[6]

Obviously, the whole case for the authorship of the man from Stratford rests upon wild speculations and the flimsiest of evidence, namely, the resemblance of his name to that printed in the First Folio and Ben Jonson's reference to the author as the "Swan of Avon," whom neither he nor other poets were previously aware of if we can judge by their unanimous silence at the time of his death in 1616. This one fact alone, the roaring silence of all the contemporary literary artists, should cause the most enthusiastic Stratfordian to stop, look, and *listen*.

Charles Dickens declared: "The life of William Shakespeare is a fine mystery, and I tremble every day lest something should turn up."[7] Well, something has turned up, if not to cause Dickens to tremble, at least to disturb the complacency of those who have a vested interest in maintaining the Stratford legend.

In 1895 Wilbur Ziegler published a novel under the title *It Was Marlowe: A Story of the Secret of Three Centuries*, which suggested that Marlowe, Raleigh, and the Earl of Rutland wrote the works attributed to Shakespeare.

In 1901 T. C. Mendenhall published an article in the December issue of *The Popular Science Monthly* which showed an amazing similarity between the literary styles of Shakespeare and Marlowe.

In 1951 Sherwood E. Silliman, a lawyer living in Scarsdale, N. Y., registered in the Copyright Office a fanciful play, *The Laurel Bough*, based on the theory that Christopher Marlowe, the Elizabethan dramatist whose plays in blank verse immediately preceded the works of William Shakespeare, did not die an early death in 1593, as commonly believed, but by the help of a clever and influential woman managed to foil his would-be murderers and live to continue his writing under the pseudonym of Shakespeare. Mr. Silliman's play was published in 1956 (see Appendix X).

Calvin Hoffman, an American poet and playwright, after more than twenty years of research, has uncovered a mass of new evidence on this controversial issue; all of which points in but one direction, namely, to the authorship of Christopher Marlowe. In a book entitled *The Murder of the Man Who Was Shakespeare,* first published in 1955 and then re-edited and republished in 1960, Calvin Hoffman presents this new evidence in logical and convincing order.

It was the argument of this book which several years ago brought about the permission of an English court to open the tomb of Sir Thomas Walsingham, the patron of Christopher Marlowe, in Chislehurst, England, news of which was widely heralded in the public press. The court's permission, however, allowed only the examination of the ornamental enclosure above the crypt. No papers were found among the quantities of sand uncovered, but obviously none should have been expected. Pharaoh Akhnaton's famous *Ode to Aton* was not found in the entrance of his tomb but inside his coffin. Permission must eventually be obtained to examine the coffins in the Walsingham crypt. If this archeological investigation is worth doing at all, it should be done thoroughly.

Over fifty candidates for the authorship of the Shakespearean works have been seriously suggested during the past century, including Queen Elizabeth I.[8] Any list of the leading candidates at the present time would probably include at least the names of Francis Bacon, Edward de Vere—Seventeenth Earl of Oxford—the Sixth Earl of Derby, and Christopher Marlowe. Is there any logical way of narrowing this list? The author believes there is. Here are some relevant questions which must be asked.

1. If any of these candidates has left behind any verse bearing his own name, how does such poetry compare with the quality of the verse to be found in the First Folio? Does it display the same level of poetic genius and imagination?

2. Is there any objective method of identifying the literary style of a given author apart from the subjective judgment of the investigator so that the literary styles of various authors of the Elizabethan era may be scientifically compared with that of the First Folio? In short, is there such a thing as a literary fingerprint which may help in identifying the real author of the Shakespearean work?

3. Finally, what was the historical context that not only made it desirable but absolutely necessary for the author to hide behind a pseudonym, the use of which was not merely temporary but was so carefully guarded even beyond the date of the author's death that it has remained a mystery until our own time? Many an author has used a pseudonym but has been ready enough to identify himself after his work has brought fame and recognition. Obviously, the author of the Shakespearean works had an adequate reason for not identifying himself, even after several of his literary offerings had been widely acclaimed. It must have been a matter of life and

17

death. What were the circumstances and attitudes of the age in which the author lived which could account for such a compelling motivation to conceal his real name?

These are the questions which the following chapters will attempt to answer.

Chapter II

SHAKESPEARE AND MARLOWE COMPARED

What poet of the Elizabethan era is it whose known works display the same kind of literary genius to be found in the First Folio? The orthodox scholars seem to be in little doubt. It is not Bacon, Edward de Vere, the Sixth Earl of Derby, or any other writer publishing works in his own name, who has been compared so favorably and enthusiastically with the author of the First Folio as Christopher Marlowe.

John Ingram wrote:

> To the date of his death and indeed for some years after, Marlowe was evidently more esteemed as a poet and more beloved as a man, than ever Shakespeare himself.[9]

Charles Dilke wrote:

> Marlowe was the most famous poet of the Elizabethan age.[9]

R. L. Ashurst wrote:

> Marlowe was by far the greatest and strongest of Elizabethan dramatists. He had a powerful influence in the mental development of the poet we know as Shakespeare.[9]

Thomas M. Parrott wrote:

> Without Marlowe there would never have been the William Shakespeare we know.[9]

Robert M. Theobald wrote:

> Marlowe's tones are to be heard in even the most advanced of Shakespeare's plays. There is an organic relation between Marlowe and Shakespeare, which requires explanation. There is an audacity about Shakespeare's diction, which comes by direct descent from Marlowe.[9]

Robert A. Law wrote:

> No sufficient reason has yet been advanced for discarding the long accepted belief that Marlowe, at his death in 1593, was a dramatist and poet of far greater repute than was ever William Shakespeare.[9]

William Allan Neilson wrote:

> Born in the same year as Shakespeare, Marlowe left behind him at 29 years of age surpassing dramatic work. In the vastness and intensity of his imagination, the splendid dignity of his verse, and the dazzling brilliance of his poetry, Marlowe exhibited the greatest genius that had appeared in the English Drama.[9]

John Bakeless wrote:

> Though Marlowe had so few models of his own, it is doubtful whether any other English writer, except Shakespeare, has ever served as a model for so many of his fellows and successors; and no one even among the Elizabethans owed more to Marlowe than Shakespeare himself. In seven of his plays Shakespeare is clearly and probably consciously copying Marlowe and in eleven other plays there are faint traces and suggestions of Marlowe's influence. The exact relationship of these two major figures is one of the chief puzzles of literary history. That it existed—that it was very far-reaching in its effect upon Shakespeare and through him upon all English letters ever after, there is no possible room for doubt. . . . Did Marlowe and Shakespeare know one another intimately? It is hard to doubt it, but it is equally impossible to prove it.[10]

Many of the plays included in the First Folio have been attributed to Marlowe in whole or in part by scholars who accept his alleged murder in 1593.[11]

Titus Andronicus

Edmund Malone: "Written by Christopher Marlowe." William Hazlitt: "Marlowe has a much fairer claim to be the author of *Titus Andronicus* than Shakespeare . . . from internal evidence." F. C. Fleay, too, attributes *Titus Andronicus* to Marlowe.

Richard III

S. S. Ashbaugh: "There is far more of Marlowe than of Shakespeare in *Richard III*." F. C. Fleay: "*Richard*

III bears strong internal evidence of Marlowe's craftsmanship." Jane Lee: "*Richard III* is full of . . . Marlowe's soul and spirit."

Richard II

A. W. Verity: "*Richard II* was written on a model furnished by Marlowe." Sir Sidney Lee: "*Richard II* was clearly suggested by Marlowe's *Edward II*."

Henry VI (Parts I, II, III)

Alexander Dyce: "There is a strong suspicion that the plays are wholly by Marlowe." Ashley Thorndike: "Marlowe's influence, if not his hand, is dominant." Algernon Swinburne: "Marlowe was more or less concerned in the production of these plays."

Among those who suggest Marlowe as the author of either one or all of these plays are A. W. Verity, Felix Schelling, Edmund Malone, Richard Farmer, and George Chalmers.[11]

As a matter of fact, more than half the works of William Shakespeare have been credited in whole or in part to the authorship of Christopher Marlowe by scholars who take for granted that Marlowe died in 1593. And yet how could this be possible when all of these works were *first* published after the date of his alleged death, and many 30 years thereafter, unless Marlowe himself was not really murdered in 1593 but was murdered in name only? In the light of such a possibility, surely the rumors and records of his early death should be critically re-examined.

Chapter III

MARLOWE'S LITERARY FINGERPRINTS

In evaluating the life and work of any author it is important to determine the span of his productive years lest any major contribution of his be accidentally or arbitrarily excluded from the Canon of his literary offerings. This is especially true in the case of Christopher Marlowe, whose death has been shrouded in mystery for several centuries and still is.

Christopher Marlowe, the son of a shoemaker, was born in Canterbury, England, early in February, 1564, for there is a church record of his being baptized February 26, 1564. He was given a scholarship to attend the Cathedral School in Canterbury, another scholarship to enroll in Corpus Christi College of Cambridge University where he earned a B.A. degree, and still another to obtain a Master's degree. His first plays were produced in London soon after he left Corpus Christi.

The works ascribed to Marlowe by orthodox scholars include the following:

Plays

Tamburlaine
Tamburlaine, Part II
Dr. Faustus
The Jew of Malta
Edward II
The Tragedy of Dido
The Massacre of Paris

Lyric Poems

The Passionate Shepherd to His Love
Description of Seas, Waters, and Rivers

Translations

Ovid's *Elegies*
The First Book of Lucan's *Pharsalia*

Epic Poems

Hero and Leander (First and Second Sestiads only)

Thomas Walsingham, the inheritor of Scadbury Park, a large estate in Chislehurst, Kent, admiring Marlowe's brilliancy, became his patron and was proud to introduce him to the court circles in which he freely moved, both on his own account and because his cousin, Sir Francis Walsingham, was the Queen's Secretary of State. Soon thereafter Marlowe was invited to join a group of intellectuals centering around Sir Walter Raleigh, most of whom were inclined to heretical views in religion.

It was Marlowe who introduced sonorous blank verse

to the English world, and he was the first to free his dramas from the previously imposed unity of time, place and action. He was widely hailed as the most gifted and original playwright of his time.

And then he wrote a pamphlet opposing the Doctrine of the Trinity. At any rate he was accused by Thomas Kyd, a former roommate, of having written it. The pamphlet had been found in Kyd's possession when his room had been searched. Kyd was arrested on May 12, 1593. The pamphlet was described in the official records as "vile heretical Conceits denying the deity of Jesus Christ our Saviour found amongst the papers of Thomas Kyd, prisoner . . . which he affirmeth that he had from Marlowe."[12] The wrath of the investigators now turned against Marlowe. The acclaim that once was his suddenly ceased and execration came instead. Eventually he was arrested at the home of Thomas Walsingham and held over for investigation by the Privy Council, but powerful friends were able to get him out on bail. The Minutes entered in the MS. Register of the Privy Council, dated May 20, 1593, read as follows:

> This day Christopher Marlowe of London, Gentleman, being sent for by warrant from their Lordships, hath entered his appearance accordingly for his indemnity therein, and is commanded to give his daily attendance on their Lordships till he shall be licensed to the contrary.[13]

Later on, while still out on bail, Marlowe was formally charged with heresy by one Richard Baines (see Appendix IV). Not long after the date of his original arrest, there were rumors that Marlowe had been killed in some kind of a brawl; and although these rumors were vague as to details of date, place and circumstance, it was widely believed that Marlowe was dead.

In 1820 James Broughton discovered the following record in the Register of Burials at the Church of St. Nicholas, Deptford, England: "1st June, 1593, Christopher Marlowe slain by Francis Frizer." The location of the grave is not mentioned.

In 1925 Leslie Hotson discovered the original report of the Coroner's Inquest concerning the alleged slaying of Marlowe, together with a postscript of his slayer's pardon, signed by Queen Elizabeth (see Appendix I and II). In this report the date of the slaying is given as "the 30th day of May, 1593," and the name of the slayer as "Ingram Frizer."

Now the point at issue is not whether the slaying took place on the 1st of June or the 30th of May, 1593, or whether the slayer was named Francis or Ingram Frizer; but rather, whether it was Marlowe who was slain or someone else, erroneously—or even intentionally—identified as Marlowe.

The Queen's Coroner was called in rather than the local coroner. The Queen's pardon for the confessed slayer was forthcoming in less than a month in an age when it was customary to delay much longer in such matters. Earlier, the Queen's Privy Council had intervened in behalf of Marlowe when they ordered Cambridge University to grant him the degree it had been withholding from him because of its own suspicion of subversive activities on his part (see Appendix III).

Therefore, it is not unreasonable to assume that the Queen's authority was here being used once more in his behalf. However, it is not necessary to make this assumption. It is not even necessary to assume that the confessed slayer actually did any slaying in this instance; only that he and his two companions falsely identified the badly mutilated body of some unknown seaman or wanderer found already murdered on the Deptford waterfront and then told a plausible "cock and bull" story to support their identification. There is no record that any of the living relatives of Marlowe had been called in to identify the body that was buried in the churchyard of St. Nicholas, or were even present at the burial. The alleged slayer and his two companions were in the employ of Thomas Walsingham at that time as confidential agents. There is documentary evidence that all three were in his employ for years thereafter.

Is it likely that Marlowe's patron would have connived in his murder, or is it more likely that he cooperated to provide his protege a way of escaping the real and immediate peril he faced at that time—the peril of being burned at the stake? The authenticity of the Coroner's Report has been questioned by scholars for various reasons (see Appendix IX).

There is considerable evidence for holding that Marlowe must have survived the date of his alleged murder by several years—enough years to produce under the pseudonym of "William Shakespeare" all the plays and sonnets which have hitherto been attributed to the actor, William Shakespeare, of Stratford-on-Avon.

As part of the evidence, this chapter would stress the

importance of the "Fingerprint Method" of identifying an author's literary style, a discovery made by Dr. Thomas Corwin Mendenhall, a distinguished scientist, at one time Professor of Physics in Ohio State University, later President of Rose Polytechnic Institute in Indiana, and in 1889 elected President of the American Association for the Advancement of Science. His discovery was first reported in *Science* for March 11, 1887.

Dr. Mendenhall found that if he had 100,000 words of a given author, counted the one-letter words, two-letter words, three-, four-, and plus-letter words, and then plotted the curve of their ratio one to another, he had a reliable fingerprint of that author's literary style that tended to remain constant—whether that author wrote in prose or poetry, whether he wrote of mice or men, or whether he wrote in his youth or again in his old age—and that this fingerprint differed from that of all the other authors he had encompassed in his study. Dr. Mendenhall did not claim that his method could be used to measure the literary value of a given author's style any more than a signature or physical fingerprint can be used to evaluate a person's character. No one writes his own signature in exactly the same way every time, but an expert can tell the difference between the genuine and the forged signature.

In the matter of physical fingerprints, even twins differ one from the other. Neither signatures nor physical fingerprints tell us whether a given person is rich or poor, good or bad, wise or foolish. They are merely useful in identifying the individual to whom the signatures or fingerprints belong. So with the method discovered by

Dr. Mendenhall. It is merely useful for the purpose of identifying an author's style, not evaluating it.

Dr. Mendenhall was curious about certain anonymous editorials which appeared in the *New York Herald* when James G. Blaine was a candidate for the Presidency of the United States. A niece of Mr. Blaine was the author of several books widely read at that time. Dr. Mendenhall applied his method in studying the anonymous editorials and the known works of this niece and found the ratio-curves in both to be identical.

Dr. Mendenhall laid aside his work and turned to other interests. But in 1901 a wealthy Bostonian, Augustus Heminway, firmly believing that Francis Bacon must have written the works attributed to Shakespeare, employed Dr. Mendenhall to use his method in an examination of the major literary offerings of the Elizabethan period with the hope, of course, that the results would establish the authorship of Bacon. Dr. Mendenhall reported his findings in *The Popular Science Monthly* for December, 1901, under the title "A Mechanical Solution of a Literary Problem." Just a few months before his death in 1924 he made a later report in the form of an illustrated lecture in the First Unitarian Church of Cleveland, Ohio. It was my good fortune to hear that lecture and to participate in the question period which followed.

Dr. Mendenhall told about studying the works of Ben Jonson, Oliver Goldsmith, Francis Beaumont-John Fletcher, Christopher Marlowe, Lord Lytton, Joseph Addison, and of course the First Folio that bears the name of William Shakespeare. He explained how a special machine was devised to record the counting, how the

29

women employed to do the counting were not permitted to work more than five hours a day because of the monotony of the work, and how no ratio-curves were plotted until all the counting had been completed, checked and double-checked for accuracy.

He declared that all American and British authors he had examined go up to their highest point in the use of three-letter words, the highest point differing, of course, with each individual author. The exceptions to this were John Stuart Mill, who reaches his highest point in his use of two-letter words, and both Shakespeare and Marlowe, who reach their highest points in the use of four-letter words, as well as Beaumont and Fletcher who jointly do also.

Among the words counted there were 200,000 from Bacon's *Advancement of Learning* and his prose history of Henry VIII, and a number of short essays; all the words from the plays commonly accepted as Marlowe's; 400,000 words from the plays, prose and sonnets attributed to Shakespeare; 75,000 words from the plays of Ben Jonson; and more than a million words from the other authors above mentioned.

The results showed that the ratio-curves of the works of Bacon and the works attributed to Shakespeare differed widely. The wealthy Baconian was naturally disappointed, but there was one author of that period whose known works showed a ratio-curve identical with that of Shakespeare—namely, Marlowe.

This is what Mendenhall said in his report in *The Popular Science Monthly* of December 1901, page 105:

It was in the counting and plotting of the plays of Christopher Marlowe, however, that something akin to a sensation was produced among those actually engaged in the work. . . . In the characteristic curves of his plays Christopher Marlowe agrees with Shakespeare as well as Shakespeare agrees with himself.

Now in his published report, Dr. Mendenhall, as a scientist, did not claim that his method necessarily proved anything; but it did suggest that Bacon could *not* have written these plays attributed to Shakespeare and that Marlowe could have done so under the pseudonym of Shakespeare. If Marlowe and Shakespeare were not one and the same person, then this is the only instance of two authors possessing identical ratio-curves thus far discovered, and many British and American authors have already been examined.

In the lecture which he delivered not long before he died, Dr. Mendenhall gave every impression that he, himself, was firmly convinced that his method actually proved that Marlowe and no one else must have written the plays and sonnets included in the First Folio, whatever the difficulties involved in explaining the rumors, records and reports concerning his death at the early age of 29 years.

I was so inspired by Dr. Mendenhall's lecture that later on I secured copies of the charts he had made, which are here reprinted.

Now I have examined the criticism of Dr. Mendenhall's method which has been made by H. N. Gibson in his recently published volume titled *The Shakespeare*

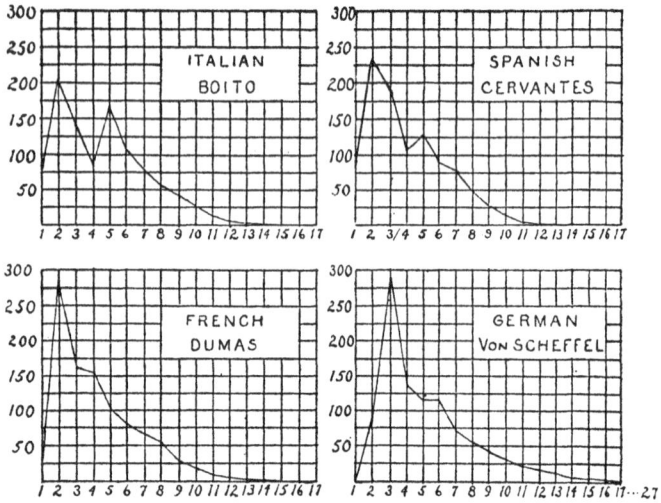

Figure 1. The ratio curves of Boito, Cervantes, Dumas, and Von Scheffel.

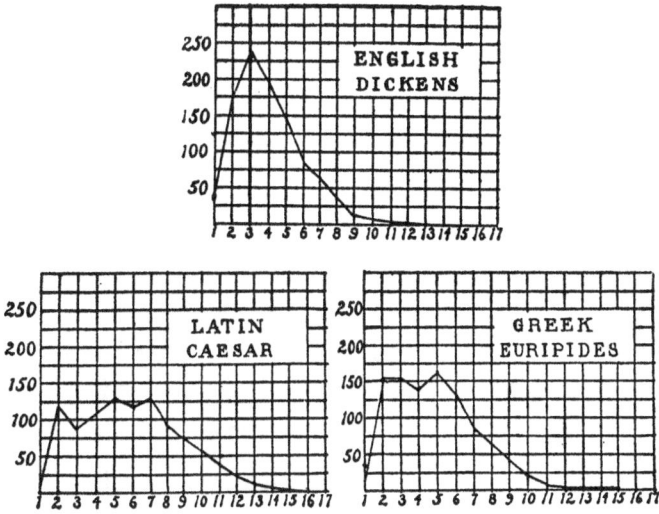

Figure 2. The ratio-curves of Dickens, Caesar, and Euripides.

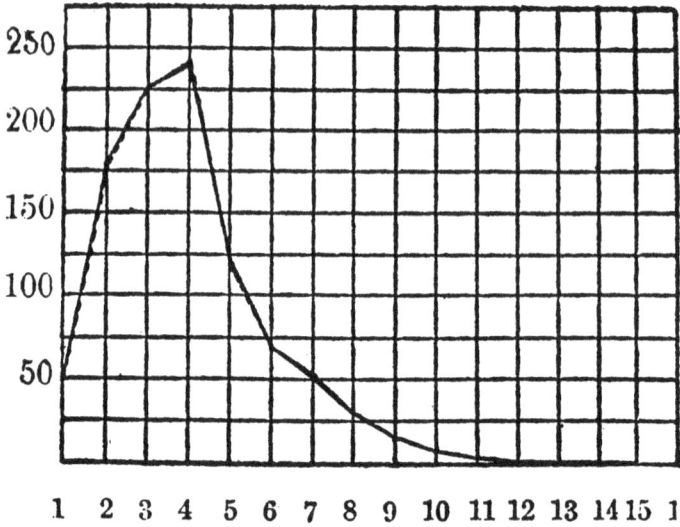

Figure 3. Shakespeare—Comparison of two groups, about 200,000 words each, showing how Shakespeare agrees with Shakespeare.

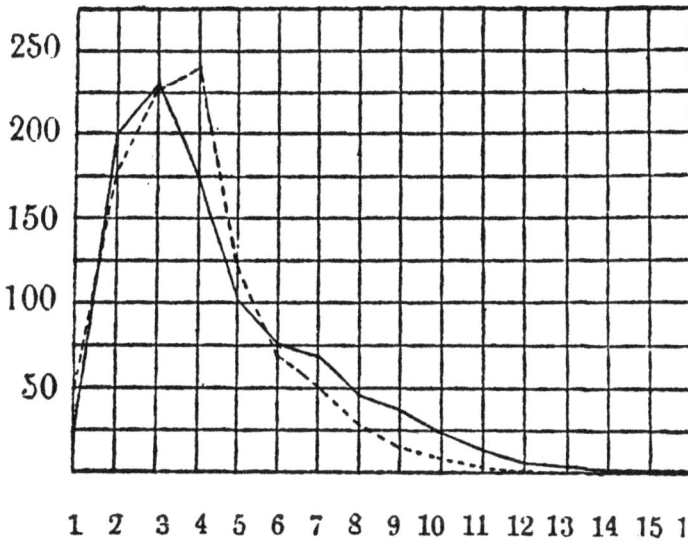

Figure 4. Bacon–Shakespeare. Dr. Mendenhall declared these to be poles apart.

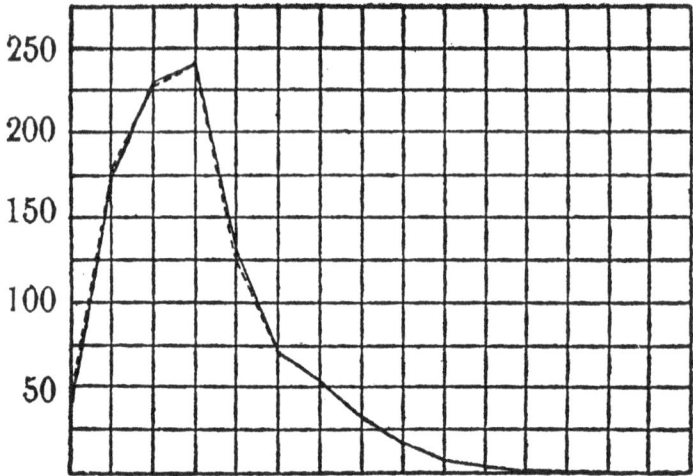

Figure 5. Marlowe—Shakespeare. Here Marlowe agrees with Shakespeare as well as Shakespeare agrees with himself.

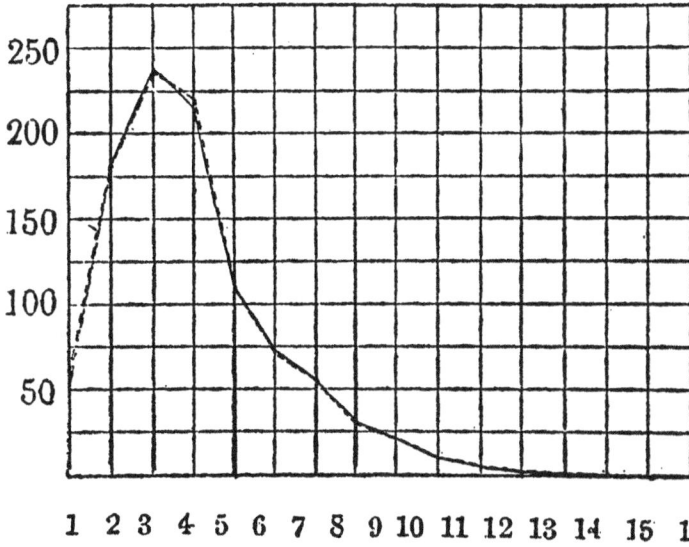

Figure 6. Two Groups, Ben Jonson, show how closely
Jonson agrees with himself.

Claimants. "A more unsatisfactory theory could scarcely be imagined,"[14] he declares and then goes on to present speculative objections to Dr. Mendenhall's method, the same kind of objections that were once used against the adoption of the Bertillon System of identifying individuals by their physical fingerprints. Mr. Gibson does not make any scientific investigation of his own to dispute the findings of Dr. Mendenhall. Until such a scientific re-investigation has been made, we may well believe that Dr. Mendenhall has left a valuable key for solving the problems of disputed authorship which have hitherto perplexed the literary world.

Dr. C. B. Williams, Professor of Statistics in London's University College, reported on Dr. Mendenhall's study in the December 1956 issue of *Biometrika*, Vol. 43, parts 3 and 4. He declared: "That Mendenhall appreciated the difference between the statistical method and evidence based on selected phraseology believed to be characteristic is clear from the following quotations: 'The chief merit of the method consisted in the fact that its application required no exercise of judgment'; and that 'characteristics might be revealed which the author could make no attempt to conceal, being himself unaware of their existence'; and again 'the conclusions reached through its use would be independent of personal bias, the work of one person in the study of an author being at once comparable with the work of any other'."

Yes, herein lies the chief merit of Dr. Mendenhall's method. It does not depend upon the exercise of judgment on the part of the investigator, but only upon the accuracy of his counting, which can be rechecked by any other investigator. Let us keep in mind that Dr. Mendenhall was employed by a Baconian, not a Marlovian. That the ratio-curve of the First Folio is identical with that of the known works of Marlowe is substantial evidence that Marlowe actually did survive the date of his alleged slaying and that he lived long enough thereafter to give us at least the plays and sonnets included in the First Folio, and even other literary offerings not so included, such as *Pericles.*

Chapter IV

MARLOWE'S RELIGIOUS HERESY

We have an "incriminating" literary fingerprint point-
ing to Marlowe as the author of the First Folio. But do we
have an adequate motive for his use of a pseudonym? It
seems to me that the answer should be obvious. Marlowe
had been charged with religious heresy at a time when
conviction meant almost certain death. Whether he or
his patron chose the pseudonym of "William Shakespeare," or whether there was a working agreement with
the actor William Shakespeare from Stratford-on-Avon
to use his name as a protective device, is not clear and, at
this point in the argument, is of subordinate importance.
The choice before Marlowe was a matter of life or death,
for to risk conviction on the charge of heresy was to risk
being burned at the stake—just as Francis Kett, also of
Corpus Christi College, had been convicted and burned
only a short while before.

Marlowe had undoubtedly been given scholarships at
Corpus Christi College with the idea of preparing him for
the Christian ministry. But because he possessed a ven-
turesome and inquiring mind, when he came to examine
the claims of religion he felt obliged to take essentially

what we would call today a liberal or Unitarian position. There is documentary evidence to show that he was accused of writing a pamphlet against the Doctrine of the Trinity in which he rejected such orthodox teachings as the Virgin Birth, the Deity of Jesus, and the Verbal Infallibility of the Bible. We do not possess a copy of that pamphlet but its substance can be inferred from Thomas Beard's *Theatre of God's Judgments,* published in 1597, and from Richard Baines' *Report of Marlowe's Blasphemies,* which was received by the Queen's Privy Council on May 29, 1593 (see Appendixes VIII and IV).

Let us bear in mind the age in which Marlowe lived. It was a time of vast religious upheaval both in Great Britain and on the continent of Europe. The theological struggle then going on, not only between Protestants and Catholics, but also between Protestants and other Protestants, was comparable in violence and intolerance to the ideological struggle going on today between the Communist and non-Communist worlds as well as within the ranks of Communism itself.

In the sixteenth century, Christians who differed slightly from other Christians were called heretics and even atheists. In 1555, Hugh Latimer and Nicholas Ridley were put to the torch for their religious convictions. In the following year, Thomas Cranmer, Archbishop of Canterbury, was condemned for heresy. Even his high office, which crowned the heads of England's monarchs, could not save his own head. He, too, was burned at the stake. In 1593, when Marlowe was charged with being both a heretic and an atheist, this cruel spirit of religious intolerance was still in full force. Knowing what had happened to Latimer, Ridley, Cranmer, and scores of others similarly charged, including Francis Kett in 1589, Marlowe would naturally desire to avoid paying the price of martyrdom for his convictions if at all possible. He undoubtedly was a heretic, but he was obviously not an atheist.

In *Doctor Faustus* he clearly reveals his own faith in a divine moral order in which men are punished by their sins, not for them. Even in *Tamburlaine, Part II*, where Tamburlaine defies Mohammed by ordering his soldiers to burn copies of the Koran within the gates of Babylon, it is not God but merely a man-made god who is defied (see Appendix VII).

> Tamburlaine:
> "Wel souldiers, Mahomet remaines in hell.
> He cannot heare the voice of Tamburlain,
> Seeke out another Godhead to adore,
> The God that sits in heaven, if any God,
> For he is God alone, and none but he."

In these lines Marlowe was believed by some of his contemporaries to be voicing his own theological views and was charged with being an atheist, but today he would not be so charged by many of our theologians. If he were living today, instead of being arrested, he probably would be offered a chair in one of our leading theological seminaries. In his day, however, a man with his liberal beliefs and a record of having declared them was in mortal danger.

He had to flee for his life, and the deception at Deptford provided by confidential agents of his powerful patron, Thomas Walsingham, was the only course open to him to escape the awful predicament he was in; then to go into voluntary exile, perhaps to journey on the continent of Europe as far as Italy; and later on, after the fury against him had subsided, return to England and there, under the pseudonym of Shakespeare, continue his literary labors.

In fact, in his prologue to *The Jew of Malta,* published forty years after the date of his alleged murder, Marlowe declares that this is precisely what took place:

> Albeit the world think Machevil is dead,
> Yet was his soul but flown beyond the Alps,
> And now the Guize is dead, is come from France
> To view this land and frolic with his friends.
> To some, perhaps my name is odious,
> But such as love me guard me from their tongues,
> And let them know that I am Machevil,
> And weigh not men and therefore not men's words:
> Admired I am of those who hate me most.
> Though some speak openly against my books
> Yet will they read me, and thereby attain
> To Peter's Chair: and when they cast me off,
> Are poisoned by my climbing followers.
> I count religion but a childish toy,
> And hold there is no sin but Ignorance,
> Birds of the air will tell of murders past;
> I am ashamed to hear such fooleries. . . .
> But . . . I come not, I,
> To read a lecture here in Britain,
> But to present the tragedy of a Jew . . .
> I crave but this, grace him as he deserves,
> And let him not be entertained the worse
> Because he favors me.

Surely this is the author speaking about himself. Robert Greene, a contemporary poet, had called Marlowe "Machiavellian."[15] Hence Marlowe's slanted reference to himself as "Machevil." The Duke of Guize was the prosecutor of the heretical Protestants in Marlowe's drama *The Massacre of Paris*. Richard Baines who had originally charged Marlowe with heresy died not long thereafter. Here then is the author declaring that since his prosecutor has died, he—Marlowe "is come from France to view this land and frolic with his friends." Note especially the lines:

> To some, perhaps my name is odious,
> But such as love me guard me from their tongues.

Again note:

> Birds of the air will tell of murders past;
> I am ashamed to hear such fooleries. . . .

Here the author seems to warn his friends that his real name can no longer be mentioned aloud and to deny that he had any part in the deception that took place at Deptford.

The only deception it is necessary to charge against Marlowe is the use of a pseudonym. But many a religious heretic of that same period hid behind such a protective device. To mention but a few among the many:

> David Jorvis as John of Bruges
> Paola Ricci as Camillus Renatus
> Sebastian Costellio as Martin Bellius

Bernadino Ochino as Antonius Corvinus
Casper Schwenckfeld as Eliander
Michael Servetus as Michael Villeneuve[16]

When Michael Servetus, the Spanish priest, was branded as a heretic early in his career, by John Calvin of Geneva, for denying the Doctrine of the Trinity, he escaped to Paris, changed his name to Michael Villeneuve after his native city in Spain, temporarily abandoned his theological pursuits, and prepared himself for a career in medicine. Years later he served as physician to the Roman Catholic Bishop of Lyon. Eventually, he was able to resume his old interest in theology. He wrote a book, *The Restoration of Christianity,* in which he argued in greater detail against the unscriptural Doctrine of the Trinity. His book was published anonymously, but Servetus could not resist the temptation to identify himself; so he put the initials of his name in small capitals— M.S.V. (Michael Servetus of Villeneuve)—just before the word "Finis" in the last chapter of his book. John Calvin, his theological adversary in Geneva, noticing these initials, jumped to the correct conclusion that Dr. Michael Villeneuve was but the pseudonym for Michael Servetus, the former heretic. Under the assumed name of William Laye, Calvin wrote to inform the Catholic Inquisitor in Lyon about the presence in his city of Michael Servetus, a dangerous heretic—dangerous to both the Roman Catholic and Protestant communions. Michael Servetus was arrested and jailed. Through the help of friends he managed to escape and then threw himself on the mercy of John Calvin whom he hoped to

45

convert to his own point of view. But failing, he was finally burned at the stake, just eleven years before Marlowe was born.

By the same token it must have been an exasperating experience for Marlowe to keep from revealing his own name. Many of the Sonnets attributed to Shakespeare proclaim the sadness of a man who is obviously in exile and desperately anxious to tell the world who he really is, but not quite reckless enough to do so.

Here are excerpts from Sonnets 26, 36, and 76.

> Lord of my love to whom in vassalage
> Thy merit hath my duty strongly knit,
> To thee I send this written embassage,
> To witness duty, not to show my wit.
>
> Let me confess that we two must be twain
> Although our undivided loves are one. . . .
> I may not evermore acknowledge thee
> Lest my bewailed guilt should do thee shame
> Nor thou with public kindness honor me
> Unless thou take that honor from thy name.
>
> Why write I still all one, ever the same,
> And keep invention in a noted weed,
> That every word doth almost tell my name,
> Showing their birth, and where they did proceed?

"That every word doth almost tell my name." The name of the author is given as "Shakespeare." Obviously, this cannot be the author's real name. Surely the author and the young man he addresses, whoever he was, shared a common grief. Mr. Calvin Hoffman argues in his book,

The Murder of the Man Who Was Shakespeare, that this is Marlowe trying to comfort his patron and himself in their mutual sad fate. Mr. Hoffman quotes several other passages from the Sonnets to indicate that the author is a tortured and frustrated soul trying to tell his friends who he really is without betraying his guarded secret to his enemies and potential prosecutors.

It seems to this writer that this argument is most convincing whether Mr. W. H. is eventually identified as Walsingham, as William Hatcliffe as Leslie Hotson maintains, as Willie Hughes as Oscar Wilde has suggested, or as someone else.

In spite of the peril involved, the author's impulse to identify himself seems to have been irresistible, for in *As You Like It* there is still another instance. *As You Like It* was registered at the London Stationers' Office in 1600 with the caveat "a booke to be staid." It was not published until 1623. One of the obvious reasons was a direct reference in Act III, Scene V, to the line of Marlowe's *Hero and Leander*:

> "Dead shepherd! now I find thy saw of might,
> 'Who ever loved that loved not at first sight?'"

Furthermore, there is a character in this play bearing the name "William" who is a rustic and a simpleton. Touchstone, the Clown, says to him in Act V, Scene i:

> ". . . for it is a figure of rhetoric that drink being poured out of a cup into a glass, by filling the one doth empty the other; for all your writers do consent that ipse is he; now, you are not ipse, for I am he."

What does this mean? It has no relevance to the rest of the play, and apart from the theory of the author's attempt to identify himself, it has no meaning whatsoever. Here the author, under the guise of a clown, is telling the world that "all the writers recognize that I myself am the real author of the works attributed to you, William. You are not ipse, for I am he. I have merely emptied my cup of fame into your glass, which should be as obvious to all but simpletons as it is to those who know what it means to write creatively." Surely, here the author is protesting that his real name is not "William."

Who was capable of writing *As You Like It* and was at the same time under the agonizing necessity of having to conceal his real name? I agree with Calvin Hoffman that this is Marlowe making one more desperate but calculated effort to identify himself without endangering his own life or the lives of his friends and supporters. It is no wonder that *As You Like It*, first registered in 1600, was not published until 1623. By that time the author was probably dead, or the original charge of heresy was deemed to have been made so many years before—thirty years before—that there was little risk of its being renewed.

Even in 1623, the well-kept secret of Marlowe's authorship could not be publicly acknowledged without bringing disgrace and recriminations on those still living who had helped him in any substantial way to escape the customary penalty for his heresy.

This number could have included even highly placed churchmen who, though not holding heretical beliefs themselves, were firmly opposed to the cruel religious intolerance of the time that would persecute the heretic even to the point of death at the stake.

Thomas Walsingham, Marlowe's patron, was such a highly placed churchman—a member of the Anglican Church in Chislehurst, Kent. He had been knighted by Queen Elizabeth several years after Marlowe's arrest at Scadbury Park. Walsingham was still living when the First Folio was published and did not die until several years later, August 11, 1630.

Chapter V

ADDITIONAL ARGUMENTS AND CONCLUSION

Let us summarize some of the additional arguments of
Mr. Hoffman and others with which the author of this
volume agrees.

1. The first poem to be attributed to Shakespeare,
Venus and Adonis, appeared four months after the
alleged death of Marlowe, but it was first registered with
the Stationers' Company of London anonymously—just
a few days before Marlowe's arrest. While published
under the name of William Shakespeare, the author ex-
plicitly states that the poem is "the first heir of my invention." At any rate there is no record of any literary
offering bearing Shakespeare's name before September
1593. Thereafter, several plays reminiscent of Marlowe's
style and literary imagination began to appear, at first
anonymously and then later, when republished, under
the name of Shakespeare. But when the complete works
of Shakespeare were published for the first time in the
Folio of 1623, seven years after the death of Shakespeare
of Stratford-on-Avon, there were included 20 new plays
never before disclosed to the public. These were:

The Tempest
The Two Gentlemen of Verona
Measure for Measure
The Comedy of Errors
As You Like It
The Taming of the Shrew
All's Well That Ends Well
Twelfth Night
The Winter's Tale
King John
Henry VI, Part I
Henry VI, Part II
Henry VI, Part III
Henry VIII
Coriolanus
Timon of Athens
Julius Caesar
Macbeth
Antony and Cleopatra
Cymbeline

Why was the publication of these plays, constituting much the larger offering and the larger fame, postponed so long? Was there anything heretical in the life of the gentleman from Stratford to warrant such a postponement? On the contrary, he was a respected and respectable man who was buried under respectable religious auspices. But if Marlowe was their real author, there was an adequate reason for such postponement of publication, for these plays contained so many plagiarisms of Marlowe's known works as to proclaim his own authorship prematurely.

The argument of plagiarism can not be ignored. Granted that several authors of the Elizabethan period

51

borrowed ideas, plots, figures of speech and even whole lines from another author's works without due acknowledgment. But when we find an author whose unacknowledged debt to such a popular author as Marlowe is not only greater than his debt to any other known writer but even greater than his debt to all other contemporary writers combined, then there is reason to conclude that this author in question is not quoting from Marlowe, but is in fact Marlowe merely repeating himself. Let us keep in mind that it is the identity of Shakespeare as an author that is the mystery, not the identity of Marlowe.

There are at least two hundred instances listed by Calvin Hoffman in his book in which Shakespeare uses figures of speech, whole lines and even larger sections from Marlowe's verse, which would be entirely natural and legitimate if Shakespeare were Marlowe merely repeating himself. Here is just one example:

In Shakespeare's *The Merry Wives of Windsor*, Act III, Scene I, we read:

> "To shallow rivers to whose falls
> Melodious birds sing madrigals,
> There will we make our beds of roses,
> And a thousand fragrant posies."

In Marlowe's *Passionate Shepherd to His Love*, written while he was still a student at Cambridge University, we read:

> "By shallow rivers to whose falls
> Melodious birds sing madrigals,
> And I will make thee beds of roses
> And a thousand fragrant posies."

For these and other reasons—such as boldness of style and dramatic treatment of subjects—many scholars who accept the actor as the author of the First Folio nevertheless claim that Marlowe must have had a hand in writing from one to twenty plays included in the First Folio, none of which had been published before 1593. Others were published for the first time in 1623. Again we raise the question, how could this be unless Marlowe actually did survive the date of his alleged murder? This has been a real problem for the orthodox scholars.

2. The First Folio carried an engraving of the author which the world has known as Shakespeare (Portrait 3). In 1953 a weather-beaten portrait was found when the Master's room at Corpus Christi College was in the process of being renovated for the first time since Marlowe's residence at the College. Because it is dated 1585 and the age given as 21 (Marlowe was 21 in 1585), and because there is inscribed a couplet which reappears in different words but with the same meaning in Shakespeare's *Pericles* and again in Sonnet 73, Mr. Hoffman and others believe it is the portrait of Marlowe. At any rate the portrait now has an honored place in the main dining hall of the College and facsimiles of it are being widely circulated by the Marlowe Society of Great Britain (Portrait 4).

The bust of Shakespeare that now stands above his grave in the church at Stratford-on-Avon is not the original that stood there for more than a century, but was placed there in 1748 by John Hall, the sculptor (Portrait 2). This is a fact not in dispute.

There is ample documentary evidence that the original

was a heavy mustached figure with hands resting on a bag of grain and holding no pen in the grasp of his fingers. There are several extant copies of a book, listing representative citizens of Warwickshire, published by Sir William Dugdale in 1656, in which a brief biography of Shakespeare is given, together with an engraving of the original bust that stood above his grave. This engraving (Portrait 1) is a fact not in dispute.

What resemblance does the image printed in the First Folio (Portrait 3) bear to the original bust of the Stratford Shakespeare (Portrait 1)? None whatsoever, no more than Dwight D. Eisenhower looks like Albert Schweitzer. What resemblance to the portrait recently found in Cambridge? A very striking resemblance. It is the Cambridge student with 15 to 25 years added.

3. When Marlowe's death was rumored, most of the major contemporary poets either publicly praised and acclaimed or severely criticized and condemned him, but few ignored him. When the Shakespeare of Stratford-on-Avon died, as we have noted before, none of his literary contemporaries said a word one way or the other. His son-in-law wrote in his diary this line: "My father-in-law died on Thursday."[17]

Not until the First Folio was published seven years later did any poet pay tribute, and then we have four tributes to the works of Shakespeare but not one word showing any personal acquaintance with the man himself, except in one instance.

There is one tribute among the four which is most significant, signed merely by the initials "J. M." It seems to indicate that this poet, at least, recognizes the hoax of Marlowe's alleged early death and identifies him from the quality of his verse, even though that verse bears the name of another. He writes:

> We wondered, (Shakespeare), that thou went'st so
> soon
> From the World's stage to the Grave's tiring room.
> We thought thee dead—but this thy printed worth
> Tells thy Spectators that thou went'st but forth
> To enter with applause. An actor's art
> Can die and live to act a second part.
> That's but an Exit of mortality,
> This a Re-Entrance to a Plaudity.

The actor from Stratford-on-Avon died at the age of 52. That was not considered an early age in that century, but 29 certainly was.

In 1600 an anthology of poetry by John Bodenham was published, titled *Belvedere or the Garden of the Muses.* While none of the verses in this book are signed, there are many brief excerpts from Marlowe's *Hero and Leander* and his *Edward II,* and Marlowe is listed among the *Modern and Extant Poets* from which Bodenham made his selections. "It is odd to find him named in 1600 among the living poets instead of among the dead who are in a separate list," comments Dr. John Bakeless, author of *The Tragical History of Christopher Marlowe.*[18] It is indeed very odd. Either the anthologist had not heard the rumors of Marlowe's death in 1593 or, having heard them, had good reason to believe that Marlowe was still alive when he published his anthology, assuming of course his reliability as a witness.

It is also very odd that the actor Shakespeare, shortly

before his death in 1616, made a last Will and Testament which mentions the bequest of "his second best bed" to his wife and numerous other bequests to various individuals, but no bequest of any books, which were prized above jewels in that day, and not even the slightest reference to his proprietary rights in any of his alleged plays and sonnets which had been previously published.[19] The bequests of rings to Heming, Burbage and Condell have been interpreted not only as showing his connection with the theatre in London, which is conceded, but also as evidence of his authorship of the First Folio, since two of these beneficiaries were instrumental in sponsoring its publication several years later. But this conclusion does not necessarily follow. It should be noted that these three bequests were not in the body of the Will but were in an interlineation added some time later; whether before or after the death of the testator, no one knows. The Will was found by Joseph Green in 1747, 131 years after the actor's death in Stratford.[20]

The lack of any reference in Shakespeare's Will to his proprietary rights in the plays he is alleged to have written has been explained as due to the possibility that he had already sold the plays to the companies that produced them. "However, we find no evidence that this was so," writes Richard Bentley in *Shakespeare Cross Examination.* "On the contrary, there are the detailed records kept by Philip Henslowe who was a London theatrical producer. These records cover the period 1591 to 1609. Henslowe produced a number of the Shakespeare plays. His records show payments to actors and payments of royalties for dramatic works. Among the

Portrait 1. The original bust of Shakespeare according to Dugdale's *Antiquities of Warwickshire,* published in 1656.

Portrait 2. The present bust of Shakespeare as executed by John Hall in 1748.

Portrait 3. The Droeshout engraving in the First Folio, 1623.

Portrait 4. The portrait, dated 1585, found at Corpus Christi College in 1953, believed to be that of Marlowe, which, now restored, hangs in the main dining room of the college. See Frontispiece.

The rebuilt hall of the moated Manor House on the estate of Thomas Walsingham, Chislehurst, Kent, where Marlowe lived at the time of his arrest in 1593. Used by permission of Thomas A. Bushell and Major Marsham-Townshend, the present owner of Scadbury Park.

A view of the ancient oaks in Scadbury Park.

many names of persons to whom such payments were made are found the names of Ben Jonson, and of Chapman, Chettle, Day, Dekker, Drayton, Heywood, Marston, Middleton, Munday, Porter, Webster, Wilson, and the other leading playwrights of the time with their signatures and handwriting. But not once does the name Shaksper or Shakespeare appear."[21]

Similarly Edward Alleyn, who was Henslowe's son-in-law and partner, kept detailed records also. These records, together with his memoirs, were published in 1841 and 1843. Sir George Greenwood, in his book *The Shakespeare Problem Restated,* writes that the records "contain the names of all the notable actors and play-poets of Shaksper's time, as well as of every person who helped, directly or indirectly, or who paid out money or who received money in connection with the production of the many plays at the Blackfriars' Theatre, the Fortune, and other theatres. His accounts were minutely stated, and a careful perusal of the two volumes shows that there is not one mention of William Shaksper or Shakespeare in his list of actors, poets, and theatrical comrades."[22] Apparently the man from Stratford did not enjoy even the reputation of being much of an actor.

4. Furthermore, there is the argument based on the eight plays bearing the name of William Shakespeare which were not included in the First Folio but registered in the Stationers' Company of London or elsewhere in his name. Scholars believe that one of these, entitled *Pericles,* should be included in the Shakespeare Canon. The other seven almost all scholars reject as unworthy of inclusion. But surely the scholars must realize that when

they abandon any ascription to Shakespeare as the infallible criterion of authorship, then they open up the whole question of the authorship of the First Folio, which is precisely what is now being urged should be done.

Without that ascription, would anyone but Marlowe have been thought of as the real author, had not the rumors of his early death been already accepted as the truth? As Algernon Swinburne has so well said: "Marlowe is the great discoverer, and most daring and inspired pioneer in all poetic literature. Before Marlowe there was no genuine blank verse and genuine tragedy in our language."

Some of the verse in the rejected plays is so inferior as to be only a little better than the doggerel that appears as an epitaph over the grave in Stratford:

> Good friend, for Jesus sake forbear
> To dig the dust enclosed here.
> Blest be the man that spares these stones
> And curst be he that moves my bones.

Either the man buried there wrote that epitaph and requested its use, or some responsible member of his family sanctioned its use as an appropriate legend. In either case the epitaph tells us something about the literary caliber of the one whose remains rest beneath it. Or it suggests the reasonable surmise that its curse was deliberately devised as a temporary protection for the grave, until a less superstitious generation should arise with sufficient curiosity to look upon the literary inferiority of the epitaph as a clever invitation to do precisely what it obviously forbids.

Many attempts have been made to get permission to look into that grave but thus far none has been successful. Nothing can be done about looking into the grave of Marlowe because to this day it has not been discovered.

5. The actors—John Heming and Henry Condell—who gathered the manuscripts for the First Folio reported that they had received them with scarcely a blot on them. Creative writers did not usually write that way before the age of typewriters. A professional penman or scrivener must have been employed. When Thomas Walsingham, the patron of Marlowe, died in 1630, a scrivener was mentioned in his last Will and Testament. Now the fact that he thought enough of his scrivener to do this is of course no proof of Marlowe's survival after 1593, but it is consistent with the assumption and could explain the condition of the manuscripts which were so free from blots as to cause comment. Among the six signatures of the man from Stratford, there are three blots.

6. Sherwood E. Silliman has called attention to the comments of Queen Elizabeth about Richard II as recorded in the diary of William Lambarde (see Appendix V). She says: "I am Richard II, know ye not that?" Then referring to the author of *Richard II*, she observes: "He that will forget God will also forget his benefactors; this tragedie was played 40 times in open streets and houses. . . ."

Here we have contemporary evidence that the author of *Richard II* was known to possess very unorthodox views on religion. How could this have been the actor from Stratford who wrote in his Will, "I comend my soule into the the hands of God my Creator, hoping and assuredlie beleeving, through thonelie merites, of Jesus Christe my Saviour, to be made partaker of lyfe everlastings. . . ."[23] Who but Marlowe possessed the reputation of being an atheist, of having been the object of Queen Elizabeth's benevolence, and the poetic genius capable of having written *Richard II?* And if the author of *Richard II*, then he must have been the author of the rest of the First Folio.

Who wrote the plays and sonnets attributed to Shakespeare? As a layman, perhaps I am not entitled to an opinion; but in so far as I am entitled, let me say that I am convinced that Marlowe must have written them and no one else. I believe the case for his authorship has already been established. Marlowe is the youth of the author of the First Folio, and the author of the First Folio is the maturity of Marlowe.

I could of course be mistaken, but it seems to me that the theory of Marlowe's authorship solves more mysteries than it creates, while the Shakespearean theory creates more mysteries than it solves. It seems to me that not to be able to recognize the towering genius of Marlowe, under the sheltering tent of Shakespeare's name, is like going to the circus and missing the elephant or not noticing the "tallest man in the world" on exhibition. At any rate, since no life of Shakespeare was written until nearly a hundred years after his death, and since today we have more facts about both the man from Stratford-on-Avon and the man from Canterbury than early biographers possessed, surely the whole controversial problem of authorship should be thoroughly re-examined and reappraised.

Biblical scholars for over a thousand years insisted that the Pentateuch was wholly written by Moses, in spite of the fact that in one of the books constituting the Pentateuch, there is an account of Moses being buried on Nebo's lonely mountain. Today most Biblical scholars—Catholic, Protestant, and Jewish—agree on the multiple authorship of the Pentateuch. To reach this conclusion, it has not been necessary to locate and dig up the grave on Nebo's lonely mountain.

For over three centuries, Shakespearean scholars have insisted that the actor from Stratford-on-Avon was the author of the First Folio in spite of impossibilities, improbabilities, inconsistencies, and contradictions as glaring as any to be found in maintaining the Mosaic authorship of the Pentateuch. It is high time that today's champions of the orthodox position should re-examine their conclusions in the light of the new clues.

Let us keep in mind that it was the orthodox mind which brought about the original tragedy in Marlowe's life, and it is the orthodox mind today which is most likely to delay the vindication of his early fame.

Those who have doubted the authorship of the actor because there is no documentary record of his ever having obtained a college education or its equivalent, and for other reasons, have been accused of snobbery. This is the illogical argument "ad hominem." Surely Nathaniel Hawthorne, Ralph Waldo Emerson, Walt Whitman, John Greenleaf Whittier, Sigmund Freud, Mark Twain, Henry James, Charles Dickens, and Oliver Wendell Holmes were not snobs. All these, we re-emphasize, took the position that there was something incredible in the actor's authorship.

If the actor was not the author, who was? Both Edward de Vere and Lord Derby had the necessary education for the role and the opportunity to become acquainted with the life of the English court at first hand, because they were part of that court; but their published writings under their own names show no literary genius. What about Francis Bacon? He had the necessary education also, and published works of high literary quality under his own name, but the Mendenhall study of these writings, subsidized by an enthusiastic Baconian, eliminates him as the likely author of the First Folio. Besides, not one of these men possessed an adequate motive for concealing his authorship of the works attributed to Shakespeare. The alleged motive—that to have publicly acknowledged such authorship would have been embarrassing to each because of the high office he held in the government—does not begin to compare in adequacy with the desperate motive which Marlowe had for concealing his identity.

The execration that was heaped upon Marlowe because of his alleged atheism while he was still living was mild in comparison with the sustained vilification that took place after the rumors of his early death were widely accepted. Then he became the special target of the Puritan pulpit.

"The Puritan tide of obloquy rose slowly," writes Charles Norman in his book, *The Muses' Darling*, "but it finally overwhelmed the memory of Marlowe. Their story of a divine visitation on the man and his works carried all before it. Within a century, even writers attempting a critical estimate of his achievements were under the spell of his calumniators. The wrath finally spent itself, but the righteousness stayed. Those who had known him and might have defended him were dead; his books had all but disappeared. The outburst of Puritan wrath against Marlowe is without parallel in literature. No vile epithet was too vile for his detractors to use, yet most of them wrote only from hearsay, or merely embroidered one another's accounts, hardly one able to contain his gloating."[24]

If the authorship of the works attributed to Shakespeare had to be concealed behind a pseudonym, not only while the author was still living but also for many years thereafter, surely there were more compelling reasons for this concealment in regard to Marlowe than in regard to Bacon, Edward de Vere, or Lord Derby.

Marlowe was not the only literary genius to outwit the forces of religious intolerance by timely concealment of his true identity. In the eighteenth century François Marie Arouet adopted the same stratagem except for one difference. Instead of hiding behind his pseudonym— Voltaire—by which he was personally and widely known, he hid behind his original name at least in one instance and as citizen Arouet helped others to burn the books of the heretical Voltaire without being recognized. Some one has said, "It takes more brains to be a live prophet than a dead one." It must have taken considerable brains for Christopher Marlowe to avoid the awful fate that otherwise would have been his had he been a man of less resourcefulness.

It goes without saying that there remain many unsolved, perhaps insolvable, problems concerning Marlowe's life, his work and his associations.

If he did not die on the date of his alleged murder, when did he die? Shortly before the death of Shaksper of Stratford-on-Avon or shortly before the publication of the First Folio?

Where was he buried? If not in the churchyard at Deptford, could he have been buried in the same grave as Shaksper, or in the Walsingham crypt in Chislehurst. Or was he privately buried in some secluded spot on the Walsingham estate? A picture of a mysterious tomb on the Walsingham estate is shown in a recently published volume, titled *In Search of Christopher Marlowe*. The authors, A. D. Wraight and Virginia F. Stern, clearly suggest that this mysterious tomb may be the grave of Marlowe.[25]

Who was the Dark Lady mentioned in the sonnets, and who the rival poet? Was the rival poet George Chapman, or someone else? Was Ben Jonson a witting or an unwitting agent in furthering the hoax of Shakespeare? Did Marlowe ever meet and have a private understanding with the man from Stratford to use his name, or did the idea of involving the latter in any way occur merely as an afterthought to Marlowe's friends in order to insure their own security from prosecution as accomplices of a heretic?

The First Folio is a fine example of the printer's art. Apparently no expense was spared in getting it published. Yet there is a badly garbled section of it with pages mis-numbered and filled with numerous parentheses, used more or less indiscriminately, none of which was corrected when the Folio was republished several years later. This garbled section has been looked upon as a cryptogram concealing the real name of the author. Several attempts have been made to solve this cryptogram but no solution to date has been widely accepted. Surely with the invention of the electronic computer, the task of finding a solution should not prove too costly or too formidable.

These are merely a few of the intriguing problems awaiting further research.

The question arises as to what difference it makes who wrote the magnificent plays and sonnets. There they are to be read and enjoyed! Yes, to be read and enjoyed, but not to be adequately understood and appreciated without knowing as much as we can about the life and character of the author, who must have been acquainted with "the slings and arrows of outrageous fortune" and who wrote:

> "The time is out of joint! O cursed spite
> That ever I was born to set it right."

Why do we study the biography of any author if not to better comprehend and appreciate what he has written? For this reason, if for no other, we may be assured that the endeavor to solve the mystery surrounding the sudden disappearance of such a literary genius as Marlowe and the mystery surrounding the simultaneous and equally sudden appearance of "Shakespeare" as a literary genius of the same calibre will be carried on, until the scholars of the world have reached a more satisfactory agreement as to what must have taken place than they have to date.

I believe that the sudden mysterious disappearance of the one, and the simultaneous and equally sudden appearance of the other, were something more than coincidental. I believe that it will be eventually found that they were related as cause and effect; in short, that the heresy of Marlowe led directly to the hoax of Shakespeare.

To sum up, there is abundant evidence that during the sixteenth and seventeenth centuries it was not uncommon for heretics to use the protective device of a pseudonym since heresy was often punished by death at the stake. There is evidence that Marlowe was arrested on suspicion of heresy before official charges were made, and that he was allowed to go temporarily free on bail. There is evidence that casts considerable doubt on the authenticity of the reports concerning his alleged murder at the age of 29. There is Marlowe's confession in his *Jew of Malta*, published long after he was charged with heresy, that his own friends have been guarding his name from their tongues. There is also a confession in the Sonnets that the author is a troubled soul under the necessity of concealing his real name, which can not be "Shakespeare," because that is the name to which the Sonnets are ascribed. In Marlowe, we have at last a worthy candidate for the authorship of the First Folio. One who did possess the poetic genius to have written it. Finally, we have a fingerprint of Marlowe's literary style which is identical with that to be found in the First Folio. Granted that it would be desirable and most interesting to know more about the case of Marlowe versus Shakespeare than we do today. What more do we really need to know in order to reach a verdict beyond a reasonable doubt? It seems to me that what we already know is enough to reach such a verdict. Therefore, I feel no hesitancy in declaring: "Shakespeare, Thy Name is Marlowe!"

Hitherto, the chief difficulty in reaching such a verdict has been that scholars have accepted as a basic fact the assumption that the Coroner's Report of Marlowe's early death is authentic and then have had to explain away a multitude of other facts inconsistent with this assumption. The Report itself is a fact but its authenticity is an assumption. In the light of the multitude of other facts, this assumption must eventually be discarded and the Report recognized as part of a deliberately planned hoax deemed entirely necessary by those who planned it.

Whereas the original purpose of the hoax was to save the life of a great poet, today there are large commercial and institutional investments that have an enormous stake in the perpetuation of the hoax. Nevertheless, I make bold to prophesy that while the main celebration of the 400th anniversary of the author of the First Folio took place in Stratford-on-Avon, the celebration of the 425th anniversary may well be focused on Canterbury in Kent where Christopher Marlowe was born.

I have no illusions, however, that today's Shakespearean scholars, who have long championed the Stratford Myth, are going to abandon their championship tomorrow or even eventually. This is expecting too much of human nature. This is not the way in which progress in new ideas is usually achieved. The claim for Marlowe's authorship of the First Folio is comparatively so recent that it is still a new idea. It takes time for a new idea to be accepted. As Max Planck, the distinguished scientist, has so well observed: "A new scientific truth does not triumph by convincing its opponents and enabling them to see the light, but rather because its opponents eventually die and a new generation grows up that is familiar with it." The same observation is relevant to any controversial new truth in the areas of religion and literary criticism. It is going to take time before a heretic is widely recognized as Shakespeare, but I am confident that this recognition will eventually come because it is the only adequate solution of the mystery involved.

Appendix I

*The Report of the Queen's Coroner**

This document, dated June 11, 1593, was titled *Inquisition of Chancery* and was drawn up by William Danby, Gent., Coroner to the Household of our Lady the Queen. The following is a translation of the original version in Latin.

> Inquisition indented taken at Deptford Strand in the aforesaid County of Kent, within the verge, on the 1st day of June, 1593, in the presence of William Danby, Gent., Coroner of the Household of our said Lady the Queen, upon view of the body of Christopher Marlowe, there lying dead and slain, upon oath of . . . (there are sixteen named witnesses) who say upon their oath that when a certain Ingram Frizer, late of London, and the aforesaid Christopher Marlowe and one Nicholas Skeres and Robert Poley, on the 30th day of May, at Deptford Strand, within the verge, about the tenth hour before noon of the same day, met together in a room in the house of a certain Eleanor Bull, widow, and there passed the time together and dined and after dinner were in quiet sort together there, and walked in the garden belonging to the said house until the 6th hour after noon of the same day and then returned from the said garden to the room aforesaid and there together and in company

* Discovered by J. Leslie Hotson in London's Public Record Office in 1925, and included in his book, *The Death of Christopher Marlowe* (Cambridge, Harvard University Press, 1925; p. 38).

supped; and after supper the said Ingram and Christopher Marlowe were in speech and uttered one to the other divers malicious words for the reason that they could not be at one nor agree about the payment of the sum of pence, that is, le recknynge there; and the said Christopher Marlowe then lying upon a bed in the room where they supped, and moved with anger against the said Ingram Frizer, upon the words as aforesaid spoken between them; and the said Ingram Frizer then and there sitting in the room aforesaid, with his back toward the bed where the said Christopher Marlowe was then lying, sitting near the bed that is, near the bed and with the front part of his body near the table and the aforesaid Nicholas Skeres and Robert Poley sitting on either side of the said Ingram in such a manner that the same Ingram Frizer in no wise could take flight; it so befell that the said Christopher Marlowe on a sudden and of his malice towards the said Ingram aforethought, was at his back, and with the same dagger the said Christopher Marlowe then and there maliciously gave the aforesaid Ingram two wounds on his head of the length of two inches and of the depth of a quarter of an inch; whereupon the said Ingram, in fear of being slain, and sitting in the manner aforesaid between the said Nicholas Skeres and Robert Poley so that he could not in any wise get away, in his own defence and for the saving of his life, then and there struggled with the said Christopher Marlowe to get from him his dagger aforesaid; in which affray the same Ingram could not get away from the said Christopher Marlowe, and so it befell in that affray that the said Ingram, in defence of his life, with the dagger aforesaid of the value of 12 d, gave the said Christopher then and there a mortal wound over his right eye of the depth of two inches and the width of one inch; of which mortal wound the aforesaid Christopher Marlowe then and there instantly died.

Appendix II

The Queen's Pardon of Ingram Frizer[*]

The original is in Latin.

> . . . We therefore, moved by piety, have pardoned the same Ingram Frizer the breach of our peace which pertains to us against the said Ingram for the death above mentioned and grant to him our firm peace Provided:
>
> Nevertheless that the right remain in our Court if anyone should wish to complain of him concerning the death above mentioned.
>
> In testimony etc.,
>
> Witnesseth the Queen at Kew
on the 28th day of June.

[*] *The Death of Christopher Marlowe,* by J. Leslie Hotson (Cambridge, Harvard University Press, 1925; p. 37).

Appendix III

*Minutes of the Queen's Privy Council**

Concerning Marlowe's degree, addressed to the authorities of Cambridge University. The Master of Arts degree was granted shortly thereafter.

> Whereas it was reported that Christopher Marlowe was determined to have gone beyond the seas to Rheims and there remain, their Lordships thought good to certify that he behaved himself orderly and discreetly whereby he had done her Majesty good service, and deserved to be rewarded for his faithful dealing. Their Lordships request that the rumour thereof should be allayed by all possible means and that he should be furthered in the degree he was to take this next Commencement; because it was not her Majesty's pleasure that anyone employed as he had been in matters touching the benefit of his country should be defamed by those ignorant in the affairs he went about.

* *The Death of Christopher Marlowe,* by J. Leslie Hotson (Cambridge, Harvard University Press, 1925; pp. 57-64).

Appendix IV

Charges of Richard Baines Against Marlowe*

The following note was received by the Privy Council on May 29, 1593, and sent to Her Majesty, Queen Elizabeth.

Copy of Marlowe's Blasphemies as sent to her Highness.

A Note

Containing the opinion of Christopher Marlowe concerning his damnable opinions and judgment of religion and scorn of God's word.

That the Indians and many Authors of antiquity have assuredly written of above 16 thousand years ago, whereas Adam is proved to have lived within 6 thousand years.

He affirmeth that Moses was but a Jugler and that one Harriot, being Sir Walter Raleigh's man, can do more than he.

That Moses made the Jews to travell 11 years in the wilderness, which journey might have been done in less than one year, ere they came to the promised land, to the intent that those who were privy to most of his subtleties might perish and so an everlasting superstition remain in the hearts of the people.

---

* For facsimile of original document, see *In Search of Christopher Marlowe*, by A. D. Wraight and Virginia F. Stern (London: Macdonald and Co., 1965; pp. 308-309).

That the first beginning of Religion was only to keep men in awe.

That it was an easy matter for Moses, being brought up in all the arts of the Egyptians, to abuse the Jews, being a rude and gross people.

That Christ was the son of a carpenter and that, if the Jews among whom he was born did crucify him, they best knew him and whence he came.

That Christ deserved better to die than Barabbas, and that the Jews made a good choice, though Barabbas were both a thief and a murderer.

That if there be any God or good Religion then, it is the Papists, because the service of God is performed with more ceremonies, as elevation of the mass, organs, singing men, shaven crowns, etc. . . .

That all Protestants are hypocritical asses.

That if he were put to write a new religion, he would undertake both a more excellent and Admirable method.

That all they that love not Tobacco and Boys were fools.

That all the apostles were fishermen and base fellows, neither of wit nor worth, that Paul only had wit, but he was a timorous fellow in bidding men to be subject to magistrates against his conscience.

That he had as good a right to coin as the Queen of England, and that he was acquainted with one Poole, a prisoner in Newgate, who hath great skill in mixture of metals, and having learned some things from him, he meant, through help of a cunning stamp-maker, to coin French crowns, pistolets, and English shillings.

That if Christ would have instituted the Sacrament with more ceremonial reverence, it would have been had in more admiration.

That Richard Cholmeley hath confessed that he was persuaded by Marlowe's reasons to become an Atheist.

These things, with many other, shall by good and honest witness be approved to be his opinions and common speeches, and that this Marlowe doth not only hold them himself, but almost into every company he cometh he persuadeth men to Atheism, willing them not to be afraid of bugbears and hobgoblins and utterly scorning both God and His ministers, as I, Richard Baines, will justify and approve both by mine own oath and the testimony of many honest men, and almost all men with whom he hath conversed any time will testify the same, and as I think, all men in Christianity ought to endeavour that the mouth of so dangerous a member may be stopped.

He saith likewise that he hath quoted a number of contrarieties out of the Scriptures which he hath given to some great men who in convenient time shall be named. When these things shall be called in question, the witness shall be produced.

(signed) Richard Baines

Appendix V

Queen Elizabeth's Remarks Concerning Richard II[*]

This was recorded in the diary of William Lambarde.

That which passed from the Excellent Majestie of Queen Elizabeth, in her Privie Chamber at East Greenwich, 4' Augusti 1601, 43' reg. sui, towards William Lambarde.

He presented her Majestie with his Pandecta of all her rolls, bundells, mambranes, and parcels, that be reposed in her Majestie's Tower at London; whereof she had given him the charge 21st Jan. last past.

Her Majestie cheerfully received the same into her hands, saying, "You intended to present this book unto me by the Countess of Warwicke; but I will none of that; for if any subject of mine do me a service, I will thankfully accept it from his own hands:" then opening the book, said, "You shall see that I can read:" . . . Then she descended from the beginning of King John, till the end of Richard III . . . in the first page she demanded the meaning of *"oblata" cartae, litterae clausae, et litterae patentes.*

W. L.—He severally expounded the right meaning . . . Then she proceedeth to further pages. . . .

W. L.—He likewise expounded all these . . . which she took in gracious and full satisfaction; so her Majestie fell upon the reign of King Richard II, saying "I am Richard II, know ye not that?"

[*] *The Sayings of Queen Elizabeth,* by Frederick C. Chamberlin. (London, John Lane, 1925; p. 52 ff).

76

W. L.—"Such a wicked imagination was determined and attempted by a most unkind gent, the most adorned creature that ever your Majestie made."

Her Majestie.—"He that will forget God will also forget his benefactors; this tragedie was played 40 times in open streets and houses . . ."

Appendix VI

Ben Jonson's Tribute to Shakespeare[*]

First published in the First Folio edition.

To draw no enuy (Shakespeare) on thy name,
    Am I thus ample to thy Booke, and Fame:
While I confesse thy writings to be such,
    As neither *Man*, nor *Muse*, can praise too much.
'Tis true, and all mens suffrage. But these wayes
    Were not the paths I meant vnto thy praise:
For seeliest Ignorance on these may light,
    Which, when it sounds at best, but eccho's right;
Or blinde Affection, which doth ne're aduance
    The truth, but gropes, and vrgeth all by chance;
Or crafty Malice, might pretend this praise,
    And thinke to ruine, where it seem'd to raise.
These are, as some infamous Baud, or Whore,
    Should praise a Matron. What could hurt her more?
But thou art proofe against them, and indeed
    Aboue th'ill fortune of them, or the need.
I, therefore will begin. Soule of the Age!
    The applause! delight! the wonder of our Stage!
My *Shakespeare*, rise; I will not lodge thee by
    Chaucer, or *Spenser*, or bid *Beaumont* lye

[*] Herford, C. H. and Percy and Evelyn Simpson, ed. *The Poems: The Prose Works*, Vol. 8, of *Ben Jonson*. Oxford, 1947.

A little further, to make thee a roome:
 Thou art a Moniment, without a tombe,
And art aliue still, while thy Booke doth liue,
 And we haue wits to read, and praise to giue.
That I not mixe thee so, my braine excuses;
 I meane with great, but disproportion'd *Muses*:
For, if I thought my iudgement were of yeeres,
 I should commit thee surely with thy peeres,
And tell, how farre thou didst our *Lily* out-shine,
 Or sporting *Kid*, or *Marlowes* mighty line.
And though thou hadst small *Latine*, and lesse *Greeke*,
 From thence to honour thee, I would not seeke
For names; but call forth thund'ring *Aeschilus*,
 Euripides, and *Sophocles* to vs,
Paccuuius, Accius, him of *Cordoua* dead,
 To life againe, to heare thy Buskin tread,
And shake a Stage: Or, when thy Sockes were on,
 Leaue thee alone, for the comparison
Of all, that insolent *Greece*, or haughtie *Rome*
 Sent forth, or since did from their ashes come.
Triumph, my *Britaine*, thou hast one to showe,
 To whom all Scenes of *Europe* homage owe.
He was not of an age, but for all time!
 And all the *Muses* still were in their prime,
When Like *Apollo* he came forth to warme
 Our eares, or like a *Mercury* to charme!
Nature her selfe was proud of his designes,
 And ioy'd to weare the dressing of his lines!
Which were so richly spun, and wouen so fit,
 As, since, she will vouchsafe no other Wit.
The merry *Greeke*, tart *Aristophanes*,
 Neat *Terence*, witty *Plautus*, now not please;
But antiquated, and deserted lye
 As they were not of Natures family.
Yet must I not giue Nature all: Thy Art,
 My gentle *Shakespeare*, must enioy a part.
For though the *Poets* matter, Nature be,
 His Art doth giue the fashion. And, that he,
Who casts to write a liuing line, must sweat,
 (Such as thine are) and strike the second heat

Vpon the *Muses* anuile: turne the same,
    (And himselfe with it) that he thinkes to frame;
Or for the lawrell, he may gaine a scorne,
    For a good *Poet's* made, as well as borne.
And such wert thou. Looke how the fathers face
    Liues in his issue, euen so, the race
Of *Shakespeares* minde, and manners brightly shines
    In his well torned, and true-filed lines:
In each of which, he seemes to shake a Lance,
    As brandish't at the eyes of Ignorance.
Sweet Swan of *Auon!* what a sight it were
    To see thee in our waters yet appeare,
And make those flights vpon the bankes of *Thames,*
    That so did take *Eliza,* and our *James!*
But stay, I see thee in the *Hemisphere*
    Aduanc'd, and made a Constellation there!
Shine forth, thou Starre of *Poets,* and with rage,
    Or influence, chide, or cheere the drooping Stage;
Which, since thy flight from hence, hath mourn'd like night,
    And despaires day, but for thy Volumes light.

                                    Ben: Ionson

Appendix VII

*Tamburlaine's Defiance of Mohammed**

From *Tamburlaine, Part II*, Act 5, Scene 1.

Now *Casane*, wher's the Turkish *Alcaron*,
And all the heapes of supersticious bookes,
Found in the Temples of that *Mahomet*,
Whom I haue thought a God? they shal be burnt.

· · · · · · · · · · · · · · · · ·

In vaine I see men worship *Mahomet*.
My sword hath sent millions of Turks to hell,
Slew all his Priests, his kinsmen, and his friends,
And yet I liue vntoucht by *Mahomet*:
From whom the thunder and the lightning breaks,
Whose Scourge I am, and him will I obey
So *Casane*, fling them in the fire.

· · · · · · · · · · · · · · · · ·

Now *Mahomet*, if thou haue any power,
Come downe thy selfe and worke a myracle,
Thou art not woorthy to be worshipped,
That suffers flames of fire to burne the writ
Wherein the sum of thy religion rests.
Why send'st thou not a furious whyrlwind downe,
To blow thy Alcaron vp to thy throne,
Where men report, thou sitt'st by God himselfe,
Or vengeance on the head of *Tamburlain*,

* Brooke, C. F., ed. *The Works of Christopher Marlowe*. London, 1910; p. 128-129.

That shakes his sword against thy majesty,
And spurns the Abstracts of thy foolish lawes.
Wel souldiers, *Mahomet* remaines in hell,
He cannot heare the voice of *Tamburlain*,
Seeke out another Godhead to adore,
The God that sits in heauen, if any God,
For he is God alone, and none but he.

Appendix VIII

The Theatre of God's Judgements

By Thomas Beard, published 1597.

Not inferior to any of the former in Atheism and Impiety, and equal to all in manner of punishment, was one of our own nation, of fresh and late memory called Marlowe, by profession a scholar, brought up from his youth in the University of Cambridge, but by practice a playwright and a Poet of scurrility, who, by giving too large a swing to his own wit, and suffering his lust to have the full reins, fell (not without just desert) to that outrage and extremity, that he denied God and His son Christ, and not only in word blasphemed against the Trinity, but also (as it is credibly reported) wrote books against it, affirming our Saviour to be but a deceiver, and Moses to be but a conjurer and seducer of the people, and the Holy Bible to be but vain and idle stories and all religion but a device of policy.

But see what a hook the Lord put in the nostrils of this barking dog. It so fell out, that in London streets as he purposed to stab one whom he sought a grudge unto with his dagger, the other party, perceiving so, avoided the stroke, that withal catching hold of his wrist, he stabbed his own dagger into his head, in such sort, that notwithstanding all the means of surgery that could be wrought, he shortly after died thereof. The manner of his death being so terrible (for he even cursed and blasphemed to his last gasp, and together with his breath an oath flew out of his mouth) that it was not only a manifest sign of God's judgement, but also an horrible and fearful terror to all that beheld him.

But herein did the justice of God most notably appear, in that he compelled his own hand which had written those blasphemies to be the instrument to punish him, and that in his brain, which had devised the same. I would to God (and I pray it from my heart) that all atheists in this realm, and in all the world beside, would, by the remembrance and consideration of this example, either forsake their horrible impiety, or that they might in like manner come to destruction; and so that abominable sin which so flourished among men of greatest name, might either be quite extinguished and rooted out, or at least smothered and kept under, that it durst not show its head any more in the world's eye.

Appendix IX

Authenticity of Coroner's Report
Disputed by Shakespearean Scholars

A.

"The Coroner's inquest was a perfunctory matter . . . his story can not be accepted as a faithful account of what actually transpired . . . One who knows the anatomy and pathology of the human brain knows that it is almost impossible for death to follow immediately upon the infliction of such a wound (Marlowe's) . . . The Coroner's 'grim tale' of Marlowe's violent and untimely end, therefore, is not a true account of what happened . . . the Coroner was influenced by certain powers not to inquire too curiously into the violent death of an outcast Ismael." *

* The Assassination of Christopher Marlowe, by Samuel A. Tannenbaum (Hamden, Shoe String Press, 1962; pp. 41-43).

B.

"The discovery of the documents relating to Marlowe's death raises almost as many questions as it answers . . . Doubts persistently arise about (it) . . . The fact that Marlowe was at this time held by the Privy Council . . . makes matters still more suspicious. . . . One wonders whether he may not have been killed deliberately. . . . Frizer probably owed his easy escape to the Walsinghams for whom he was transacting business the very next day (i.e., after his pardon by Queen Elizabeth on the charge of murder) . . . There is something queer about the whole episode." *

* The Tragical History of Christopher Marlowe, by John Bakeless (Cambridge, Harvard University Press, 1942, Vol. I.; pp. 158-182).

C.

"It is surprising that the references to the event (i.e., Marlowe's murder) in the years immediately following should have been so scanty and so curiously vague or misleading. Mistakes began on the very day of the Inquest . . . Nor is there any indication in the churchyard of the place of the grave . . . Gabriel Harvey thought Marlowe died of the plague in 1593! In his 'Gorgon or the Wonderful Year'—September 18, 1595—the line, 'the great disease sternly struck home the stroke' must surely imply Marlowe's death from the plague! The more Harvey's references are considered the more enigmatic they become." *

* *Christopher Marlowe,* by Frederick S. Boas (Oxford, The Clarendon Press, 1940; pp. 277-279).

Appendix X

The Similarities of Shakespeare and Marlowe*

"A reading of Marlowe's known works shows the following characteristics found in Shakespeare:

1. Each used poetic blank verse. Although the verse changes somewhat in Shakespeare's works, it would not be difficult for a poet of Marlowe's versatility to make such change. Note the difference between his *Tamburlaine the Great* and *Edward the Second*.

2. Each wrote concerning the authority and pageantry of kings and princes.

3. Throughout the two works scholars are often used as characters in the plays.

4. Much of the same vocabulary and beautiful imagery appear in the plays of each.

5. Both dote on pomp and ceremony.

6. The same sources—Ovid and Holinshed's *Chronicles*—are used by each.

7. The complicated plots and counterplots appear in both works. Compare *Edward the Second* with the later historical dramas of Shakespeare.

8. Marlowe's characterization was often weak. The same failure is found in Shakespeare's early plays.

9. Much of the writing of each is uninteresting, but is eternally saved by the most beautiful poetic passages in the English language.

* *The Laurel Bough*, by Sherwood E. Silliman (New York, 1956, privately printed; pp. 12-13. By permission). *The Laurel Bough* is a fanciful play based on the theme that it was Audrey Walsingham, the wife of Thomas Walsingham, who was responsible for saving the life of Marlowe.

This and other circumstances lead to the theory that no two human minds could have such striking similarities. Begin with *Dido* and continue to *The Tempest* and you see one mind, one genius, developing from a youthful translator of the *Aeneid* to the mature creator of a world of perfect imagery."

References and Acknowledgments

1. Max Planck, *Scientific Biography and Other Papers*. New York, Philosophical Library, 1949.
2. Quoted by T. C. Mendenhall in "The Town of Talmadge—The Bacons and Shakespeare," reprinted from the *Ohio Archeological and Historical Quarterly*, 1923; pp. 24-25.
3. Calvin Hoffman, *The Murder of the Man Who Was Shakespeare*. New York, Grosset and Dunlap, 1960; p. xii.
4. *Ibid.*, pp. 6-8.
5. Mendenhall, *op. cit.*, p. 24.
6. *Ibid.*, p. 23.
7. Hoffman, *op. cit.*, p. xii.
8. George McMichael and Edgar M. Glenn, *Shakespeare and His Rivals*. New York, The Odyssey Press, 1962; p. 62.
9. Hoffman, *op. cit.*, pp. 120-121.
10. John Bakeless, *Christopher Marlowe—The Man In His Time*. New York, William Morrow and Co., 1937; pp. 290-291.
11. Hoffman, *op. cit.*, pp. 133-136.
12. *Ibid.*, pp. 60-61.
13. *Ibid.*, p. 64.
14. H. N. Gibson, *The Shakespeare Claimants*. New York, Barnes and Noble, Inc., 1962, 1963; pp. 143 ff.
15. In September, 1592, Robert Greene, referring to Marlowe and his alleged atheism, wrote in *Groatsworth of Wit*:

> Why shouldst thy excellent wit, His Gift, be so blinded that thou shouldst give no glory to the Giver? Is it pestilent Machivilian policy thou hast studied? O peevish folly! What are his rules but more confused mockeries, able

89

to extirpate in small time the generation of mankind . . .
The brother of this diabolical atheism is dead.

16. George Huntston Williams, *The Radical Reformation,* Philadelphia, Westminster Press, 1962. All these heretics with pseudonyms are discussed in this book. See its index.
17. Hoffman, *op. cit.,* pp. 279-280.
18. John Bakeless, *The Tragical History of Christopher Marlowe.* Cambridge, Harvard University Press, 1942, Vol. II; p. 292.
19. See Shakespeare's Will in *Shakespeare and His Rivals* by McMichael and Glenn, *op. cit.,* pp. 19 ff.
20. "Shakespeare Cross-Examination." Published by the American Bar Association *Journal,* 1961; p. 74. Supplementary notes by Richard Bentley.
21. *Ibid.,* p. 64.
22. Sir George Greenwood, K.C., M.P., *The Shakespeare Problem Restated,* (1908, 1937) p. 367.
23. McMichael and Glenn, *op. cit.,* p. 19.
24. Charles Norman, *The Muses' Darling.* New York, Rinehart, 1947; p. 243.
25. A. D. Wraight and Virginia F. Stern, *In Search of Christopher Marlowe.* London, Macdonald and Co., 1965; p. 264.

Permission has been given by Calvin Hoffman, author of *The Murder of the Man Who Was Shakespeare,* to write on his theme of Marlowe's authorship of Shakespeare's Works, and to quote from his copyrighted book.

INDEX

91

Lee, Sir Sidney, 22
Lily, John, 79
Lincoln, Abraham, 13
Lucan, 24
Lytton, Lord, 29

Macbeth, 51
Malone, Edmund, 21, 22
Marlowe, Christopher, 7, 8, 15, 16, 17, 19, 20, 21, 22, 23, 24, 25, 26, 27, 29, 30, 31, 36, 38, 39, 40, 41, 42, 43, 44, 46, 47, 48, 49, 50, 51, 52, 53, 54, 55, 58, 59, 60, 61, 62, 63, 64, 65, 66, 67, 69, 70, 71, 72, 73, 74, 75, 79, 83, 85, 86, 87
Marlowe Society, 7, 53
Marston, John, 57
Massacre of Paris, The, 24, 44
Measure for Measure, 51
Mendenhall, Thomas Corwin, 14, 15, 28-31, 35, 38, 39, 62
Merry Wives of Windsor, The, 52
Middleton, Thomas, 57
Mill, John Stuart, 30
Modern and Extant Poets, 55
Moses, 61, 73, 74
Munday, Anthony, 57
Murder of the Man Who Was Shakespeare, The, 16, 47

Neilson, William Allan, 20
Norman, Charles, 62

Ode to Aton, 16
Ovid, 24, 87
Oxford University, 13

Pacuvius, 79
Palmerston, Lord, 12
Parrott, Thomas M., 20
Passionate Shepherd to His Love, The, 24, 52
Paul, St., 74

Pentateuch, 61
Pericles, 39, 53, 57
Pharsalia, 24
Planck, Max, 68
Plautus, 79
Poley, Robert, 69, 70
Porter, Endymion, 57

Raleigh, Sir Walter, 15, 24, 73
Report of Marlowe's Blasphemies, 41
Restoration of Christianity, The, 45
Richard II, 22, 59, 60
Richard II, King, 59, 76
Richard III, 21, 22
Richard III, King, 76
Ridley, Nicholas, 41, 42
Rutland, Earl of, 15

Sayings of Queen Elizabeth, The, 76
Scadbury Park, 8, 24, 49
Scheffel, Joseph von, 32
Schelling, Felix, 22
Schweitzer, Albert, 54
Servetus, Michael, 45
Shakespeare, William, 8, 11, 12, 13, 14, 15, 19, 20, 21, 22, 27, 29, 30, 31, 34, 35, 36, 40, 43, 46, 47, 50, 51, 52, 53, 54, 55, 57, 58, 60, 61, 62, 63, 64, 65, 66, 67, 78, 79, 80, 87
Shakespeare Claimants, The, 31
Shakespeare Cross Examination, 56
Shakespeare Problem Restated, The, 57
Silliman, Sherwood E., 15, 16, 59, 87-88
Simpson, Percy and Evelyn, 78
Skeres, Nicholas, 69, 70
Sonnets, 12, 27, 46, 53, 64, 65, 66
Sophocles, 79
Spencer, Herbert, 12
Spenser, Edmund, 78
Stern, Virginia F., 64, 73

www.ingramcontent.com/pod-product-compliance
Lightning Source LLC
Chambersburg PA
CBHW051844040426
42447CB00006B/695

9 780806 530154